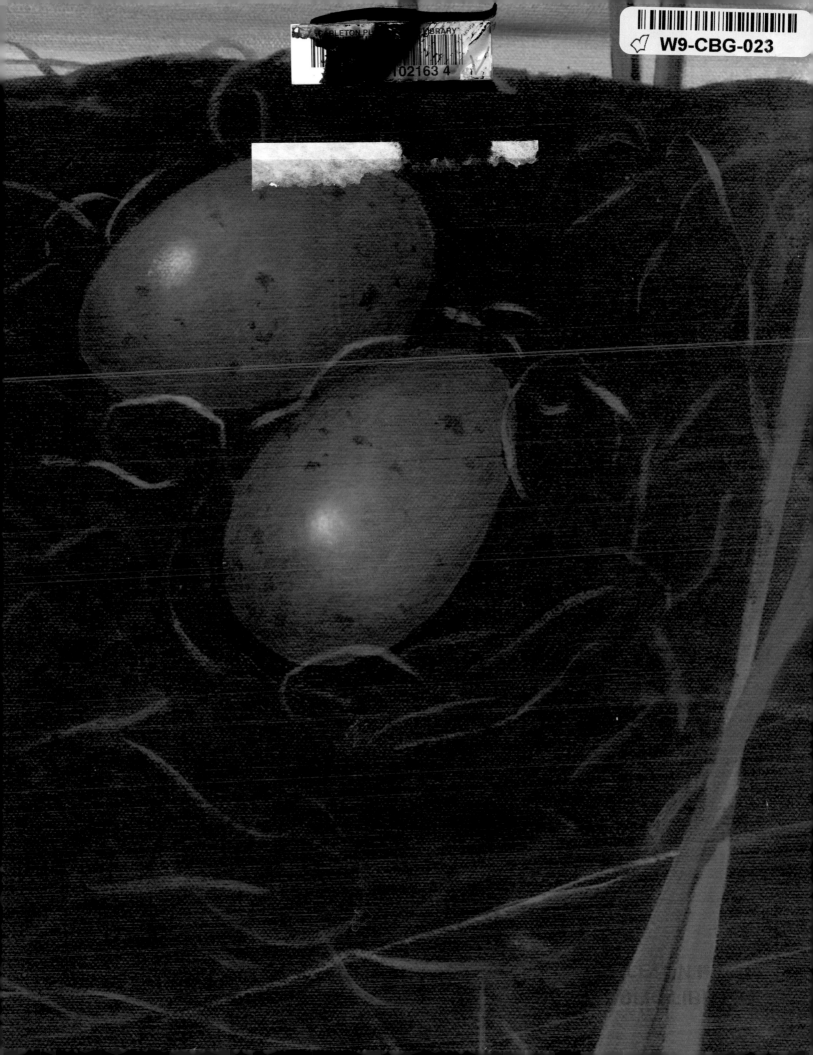

For all those who have watched, studied or written about loons, thank you. — SVG

For Tizi, Peter and all my Mill family, with thanks for seeing me through. — KR

LOON

Susan Vande Griek

Pictures by Karen Reczuch

Groundwood Books / House of Anansi Press

Toronto   Berkeley

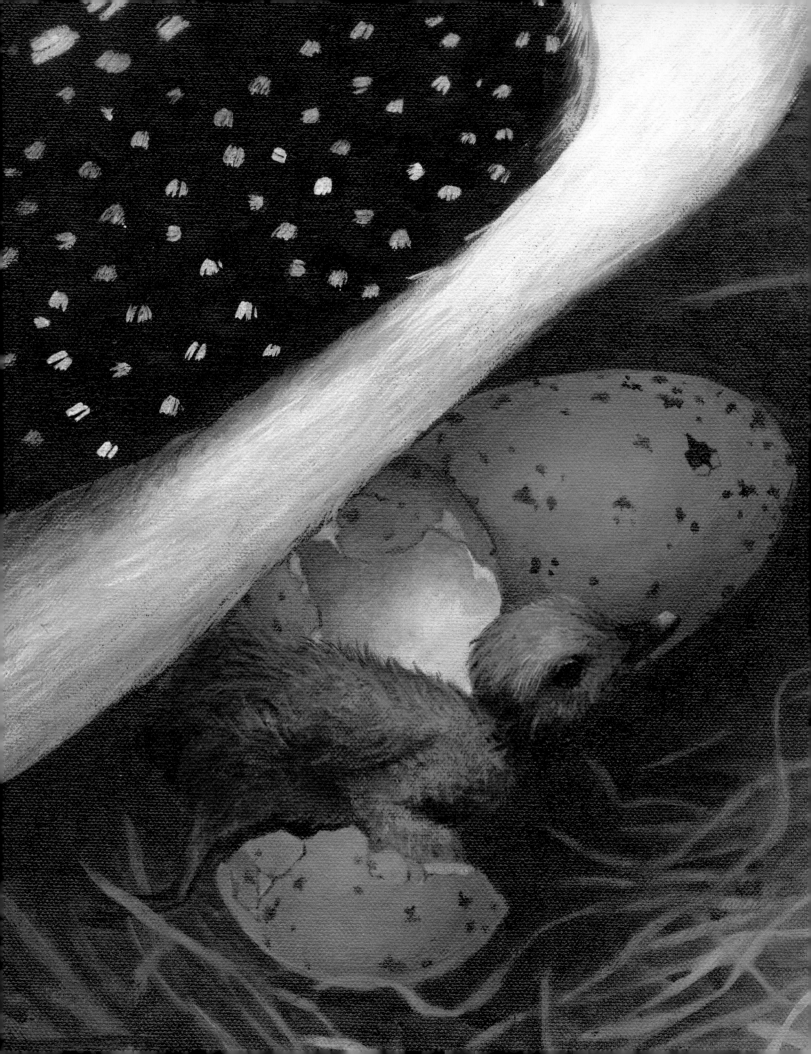

IT IS A BIRTH DAY,
a late June day,
a baby loon's first day.
From the large greenish-brown
spotted egg, in the spoon of the
waterweed-and-mud nest,
the dark little chick
pecks and peeks,
then splays out
near her mama's big webbed feet.

And less than a June day later,
she has a brother.

Two small matching loon chicks,
in darkest downy gray,
poke and peck
and pester the nest
for just one day.

Mama and Papa
have both sat
waiting,
waiting,
incubating,
listening to the lap, lap
of the lake's lullaby,
while watching for thieving weasels, gulls,
raccoons and crows.

And after almost thirty days
of trading places,
going hungry,
scrambling up on clumsy legs,
white breast to nest and ground,
Mama and Papa from the lake now call,
Follow, follow.
For a loon bird is a water bird after all.

So two little loons
plop themselves in.
Close to Mama and Papa
they float,
bob,
paddle little feet,
peep
and peer,
never left behind.

Then tired, damp and chilly,
the two chicks climb
out of the spring-cold water
and hitch themselves a ride.

On black-and-white checkered backs
they snuggle down to dry.
Sailing the lake on their loon boats
they watch the water world go by.

And look down there.
What's that? What's that?
A big bass fish,
and it's certain that a baby bird
could fit between those lips!

And there, over there.
See that? See that?
A large snapping turtle
that could put jaws round a little chick!

But the two chicks warm and settle.
And when Papa and Mama know it's safe,
they lower them into the water
where they paddle in coves and backwater shallows,
around rocks and reeds and shadows,
hooing to each other,
keeping each other close.

Papa grabs frogs and crayfish
and Mama catches snails and minnows
to slide down babies' throats.

And sometimes they doze on the water
or rest high on a feathered back,
while Mama or Papa
moves out on the lake,
fishing on their own,
away from hungry babies
who can't yet fish alone.

And one parent calls to another,
Where are you? Where are you?
Oh-hoo-oo, hoo-hoo-oo?
I am here, over here —
be back soon.

It turns summer
and it's warmer,
sunny days,
starry nights.

But danger comes slowly
paddling,
gliding across the lake.
Papa sends out a trembling
Hoo-hoo-hoo-hoo-hoo-hoo.
He dances on the water,
stands up stiff and brave,
wings tucked,
beak out,
stands as if to say,
Get back, get back.
Stay away from this place.
Do not come this way.

Then the weeks laze along,
up to ten, eleven, twelve,
and quickly and quietly
the loon chicks grow.
Their down changes to feathers,
fine feathers of paler gray.
They move out on the water,
learning their lessons day by day.

They mimic their mama
as she tips long beak and head,
dunking them underwater,
her eyes bright red,
peering in her search
for a sunfish, perch or pike.

She swoops far below her,
diving fast and deep,
so long under the surface
that a young chick might peep,
Hoo — where have you gone?
Hoo — where could you be?
She grabs herself a meal —
ah there! —
and swallows it in one piece.

The chicks copy their papa
as he pokes, picks and preens,
oiling, arranging his feathers
to keep them waterproof and neat.

And then when summer
edges into fall,
they try as he does
to fly into the air.
They run down the water,
flapping hard and long,
letting new wings take
heavy bodies, heavy bones
for a first ever bird's-eye view
of their large birth lake.

And so two loon parents,
their feathers turning back to gray,
can leave their young now
to fend for themselves
more each day.

And when fall finally grows colder
Mama and Papa fly,
going their separate ways.
They join small flocks and migrate
to a water far away,
to the sea where they will winter,
apart yet not alone,
though spring will likely bring them back
to each other and this home.

They fly,
leaving their young
to fish, dive and doze,
to grow strong
a short while longer,
until they too take flight,
before the lake water freezes
and turns to hard winter ice.

The two young loons
together run, flap,
rise
from their known watery place
to the unknown sky.

They join up with others,
their flying humpback shapes
traveling by instinct,
feet trailing behind,
over land and rivers,
over roads and trees,
to an unknown ocean,
an unknown sea.

They fly to new water,
open and vast,
without coves and weeds
or rocks and trees,
to water that's salty,
where they land and stay,
feeding on fish that swim their way.

Through the fog of winter,
the sun of summer,
they ride the waves,
sit on that sea.
For three or four years
they live on the ocean
with a loose flock of others,
drifting constantly.

They dive near shore
to fish by day
and paddle out with the night,
tucking beaks under wings,
to safely sleep,
growing older
quietly.

And then
one midwinter
their feathers molt.
Gone is the gray of back and head,
turned instead to checkered, striped, spotted
white and black.

With spring's new and lovely feathered coats,
throats necklaced and ready to call,
they stir,
they grow restless.
It's time to take off.

They are ready to parent,
ready to nest.
Each makes the long journey,
flies off from the rest
to find themselves a partner, a mate
on a quiet, faraway fish-filled lake,
to find another with which to wait
for eggs to hatch
and chicks to raise.

Each listens for
another voice
to call out
and answer
from spring to fall,
Ooh-hoo-oo, ooh-hoo-oo.
I'm here, I'm here,
out in the dark,
out on the lake.
Oh-hoo-oo, hoo-hoo-oo?
Where are you?

A Note on the Common Loon

THE COMMON LOON, with its uncommon coat and calls, is the kind of loon that most people see and hear. Its remarkable diving ability and its habitat have given this bird its other name — Great Northern Diver. Found in Canada, the northern United States, Greenland, Iceland and sometimes parts of northern Europe, it is one of five different types of loons. The others are the red-throated loon, the Pacific loon, the Arctic loon and the yellow-billed loon.

The common loon is a large bird, with strong webbed feet and legs set far back on its heavy-boned but streamlined body. These characteristics make it clumsy on land, but a powerful diver. It can swim underwater to a depth of seventy meters (230 feet), where it catches and feeds on fish and sometimes on frogs, snails and crayfish.

Loons are water birds. Except for about thirty days a year, when they are nesting, they live and feed totally on the water. Females usually lay one or two eggs, and the chicks go into the water only a day after hatching. The loon parents protect and feed them for about three months. After that the young loons can get by on their own.

Full-grown loons, ranging in age from three to thirty years, spend each spring and summer on northern lakes. The lakes must be big enough to provide fish for the loons and their families and to allow for a take-off run across the water. They must also be quiet to give the loons the privacy they need to nest and rear their chicks. The loons settle in and defend their territory, whether it is a small lake or part of a bigger one.

When the weather and water cool, the loons migrate to the sea. The older ones leave first, then the young, flying swiftly and strongly once they manage to get their heavy bodies into the air. The parents separate from each other as well, but they are very likely to return to the same lake to find one another again in the spring. Rarely, a loon will find a new mate, perhaps when one bird dies or if one male successfully challenges and takes over another bird's territory.

While they are maturing and during the winter, loons live on ice-free water, usually along the Pacific and Atlantic coasts. There they feed and rest in their immature or winter gray-brown plumage, rather silent except for a few quiet hoots.

The hoot, or hoo, is just one of the four sounds that loons make. It is used among chicks and parents to keep close track of each other. The yodel is a long call with repeating notes, which males use to defend their lake territory. What some people describe as a quivering, laughing call is the loon's tremolo. It sounds

COMMON LOON
Gavia immer

RED-THROATED LOON
Gavia stellata

like six or eight repeated, quick hoos, and it usually signals a loon's annoyance or alarm. And finally, there is the wail, a drawn-out oh-hoo that loons use to stay in contact with each other when they are apart on the lake. It is often heard at night.

Some scientists believe that the loon is a very old species of bird that may have lived on lakes and seas for millions of years. To make sure it continues for countless more, we must take better care of the loon's habitat. More and more summer cottages on more and more lakes could mean that fewer loons will settle or nest on those lakes. These birds like quiet waters to raise their young. Boating waves can flood their low-lying nests, people can scare them off their eggs, and encounters with people or boats can endanger their lives.

Environmental problems also result in fewer loons. Acid rain from air pollution changes the make-up of lake water and kills off fish, leading to fewer lakes where loons will harbor and feed. Deadly toxins in lake water, such as mercury, make their way into fish, which are then eaten by loons. Oil spills on the sea can also take the lives of these birds. Even global warming might be affecting loons. Rising temperatures could be leading to more storms, which flood more nests and create cloudy water with more algae growth. Loons need clear water to see and catch their food. Global warming can also change habitats, drying up some small lakes while causing water levels to rise in other areas, again flooding low-lying nesting sites.

Fishing is another danger. Fishing nets and lines can entangle the birds. And when people drop lead sinkers, or weights, from their lines, loons may swallow them as they take in small stones to help them digest their food. The swallowed lead kills the loons. Fortunately, in many places people have stopped using lead sinkers.

So far the common loon is not an endangered species, but the areas in which it breeds and nests have shrunk in size. It is up to us to ensure that this habitat does not get even smaller. Perhaps we can help by building fewer homes or cottages near some lake shores, and by providing floating nesting platforms for loons to use. And we can be extra careful to keep our distance when fishing, boating or swimming if we think loons are nearby.

It is only when we give them space and quiet that we might have a chance to see the beautiful black-and-white patterned backs of these birds and to hear their unique hoots, wails and yodels.

PACIFIC LOON
Gavia pacifica

ARCTIC LOON
Gavia arctica

YELLOW-BILLED LOON
Gavia adamsii

For Further Reading

Getting to Know Nature's Children: Loons by Judy Ross. New York: Grolier, 1985.

Looking for Loons by Jennifer Lloyd, illustrated by Kirsti Anne Wakelin. Vancouver: Simply Read Books, 2007.

Loon Chase by Jean Heilprin Diehl, illustrated by Kathryn Freeman. Mount Pleasant, sc: Sylvan Dell Publishing, 2006.

Loons: Loon Magic for Kids by Tom Klein. Milwaukee: Gareth Stevens, 1990.

The Loon's Necklace by William Toye, illustrated by Elizabeth Cleaver. Toronto: Oxford University Press, 1988.

Acknowledgments

I would like to acknowledge Nan Froman for her help in shaping this book. — svg.

Thanks to Mark Peck, Ornithology Collections, Royal Ontario Museum, for advice on the illustrations. — kr.

The publisher would like to thank Ron Ridout of Bird Studies Canada for checking the text.

Groundwood Books / House of Anansi Press
110 Spadina Avenue, Suite 801, Toronto, Ontario M5V 2K4
or c/o Publishers Group West
1700 Fourth Street, Berkeley, CA 94710

We acknowledge for their financial support of our publishing program
the Canada Council for the Arts, the Government of Canada through the
Canada Book Fund (CBF) and the Ontario Arts Council.

Canada Council   Conseil des Arts
for the Arts   du Canada

ONTARIO ARTS COUNCIL
CONSEIL DES ARTS DE L'ONTARIO

Library and Archives Canada Cataloguing in Publication

Vande Griek, Susan
Loon / Susan Vande Griek ; illustrated by Karen Reczuch.

ISBN 978-1-55498-077-2

1. Common loon—Juvenile literature. I. Reczuch, Karen
II. Title.

QL696.G33V35 2011   j598.4'42   C2011-901136-0

The illustrations were done in acrylic on canvas.
Design by Michael Solomon
Printed and bound in China

White-tailed Deer

Marsh Wren

Raccoon

Great Blue Heron

Yellow Perch

Smallmouth Bass